Clever Comprehension KS2

Contents   Page

A Guide to Excellent Reading	2
Paper 1	3
Paper 2	9
Paper 3	16
Paper 4	24
Paper 5	32
Answer Guide	40
Resources	61

Copyright © 2015 Miss Olubi & TheTutoress.com.

All rights reserved. This book or any portion thereof may not be reproduced or used in any matter whatsoever without the express written permission of the publisher.

A Guide To Excellent Reading

At Key Stage 2, many children find it challenging to read texts from different genres. In fact, one of the most challenging areas of learning for many children is understanding the meaning behind the texts they've read.

It's one thing to read a story and another to understand what it means. The questions in the *Clever Comprehension* series of *books* are designed to get students to think about what they've read and to assess their learning.

How can you improve your reading?

The first key to becoming a better reader is to read more. Read for at least ten minutes before you go to bed. Read for ten minutes in the morning and read for at least ten minutes before you watch a TV program or play games. By reading more often, you'll improve your ability to understand more complicated sentences, texts and stories.

Another way to improve your reading and comprehension skills is to read a wider variety of books. In other words, don't just stick to reading the same type of books all the time. For example, read a book from one genre one week and then another genre another week. In doing so, you'll begin to understand a wider variety of texts and you'll find comprehension exercises to be a lot easier.

I hope these tips have helped you to think of changes that you could make to your reading. Now get started on the following comprehensions and aim to do your best and learn from any mistakes you make.

Paper 1

Poor little Lucy
By some mischance,
Lost her shoe
As she did dance:
'Twas not on the stairs,
Not in the hall;
Not where they sat
At supper at all.
She looked in the garden,
But there it was not;
Henhouse, or kennel,
Or high dovecote.
Dairy and meadow,
And wild woods through
Showed not a trace
Of Lucy's shoe.
Bird nor bunny
Nor glimmering moon
Breathed a whisper
Of where 'twas gone.
It was cried and cried,
O yez and O yez!
In French, Dutch, Latin,
And Portuguese.
Ships the dark seas
Went plunging through,
But none brought news
Of Lucy's shoe;
And still she patter
In silk and leather,
O'er snow, sand, shingle,
In every weather;
Spain, and Africa,
Hindustan,
Java, China, and lamped Japan;
Plain and desert,
She hops-hops through,

Pernambuco to gold Peru;
Mountain and forest,
And river too,
All the world over
For her lost shoe.

The Lost Shoe by Walter De La Mare

Circle the correct answer.

1 Lucy lost her:

    a) hat   b) purse   c) shoe

1 mark

2 The word 'twas is short for:

    a) It is   b) It was   c) It has

1 mark

3 List five places where her shoe was not found.

_____

_____

5 mark

4 An adjective is a word that describes something. Find two **adjectives** that are used in the poem.

_____

1 mark

5 Explain in your own words why these adjectives are effective.

_____

_____

1 mark

6 How would you describe Lucy? Write **one** sentence to describe her. Your sentence should include at least two adjectives.

_____

_____

_____

2 marks

7 An **onomatopoeic word** is a word that sounds like itself.

E.g. **boom, bang** and **clash** are all onomatopoeic words.

Identify **one** onomatopoeic word that is used in the poem.

_____

1 mark

In your own words, explain what these phrases mean:

8 'glimmering moon'

_____

9 'ships the dark seas'

_____

10 showed not a trace

_____

11 'or high dovecote'

_____

2 marks

12 An **alliterative phrase** refers to when words that start with the same letter or sound are used together in a phrase or sentence.
E.g. **b**ossy **b**ear, **c**lean **c**arpet, **t**he **t**all **t**able.

Identify which **alliterative expression** is used in line 4.

_____

1 mark

Complete each word with '**s**' or '**e**'.

13 complim_nt
14 shingl_
15 mi_chance
16 lo_t
17 de_ire
18 a_tray
19 forgot_n
20 mi_ _ ing

8 marks

21 In your own words, summarise what this poem is about.

_____
_____
_____
_____

_____

4 marks

Idioms are popular expressions that mean something different from their actual meaning.

Using your own words, explain what these idioms mean.

(a) A penny for your thoughts

_____

(b) The ball is in your court

_____

(c) The best of both worlds

_____

(d) To bite off more than you can chew

_____

(e) It costs an arm and a leg

_____

(f) Cry over spilt milk

_____

(g) Don't put all your eggs in one basket

_____

(h) I heard it on the grapevine

_____

(i) To make a long story short

_____

(j) Take it with a grain a salt

_____

10 marks

22 Can you think of any other popular idioms? Write five below.

_____

_____

_____

_____

_____

5 marks

An **adverb** is a word that describes what someone or something is doing.
Underline the adverb in each sentence.

23 He sat silently during dinner.

24 She played roughly during playtime.

25 Joe and I go to football practice daily.

                                                                    3 marks

Match each word with its definition as used in the poem.

    26 mischance   (a) diving

    27 trace   (b) shiny

    28 glimmering   (c) sign

    29 shingle   (d) accident

    30 plunging   (e) pebbles

                                                                    5 marks

Complete each word with '**h**' or '**p**'.

31 t__ief (thief)

32 Lig__tning (lightning)

33 __ublication (publication)

34 a__ __roval (approval)

35 ham__er (hamper)

36 centi__ede (centipede)

37 s__akily (shakily)

38 __andler (handler)

39 pro__ortion (proportion)

40 __ospital (hospital)

                                                                    10 marks

7

Write the **opposite** meaning of each word.

41	beautiful _____		46	borrow _____
42	before _____		47	fade _____
43	accept _____		48	narrow _____
44	backward _____		49	correct _____
45	calm _____		50	meek _____

10 marks

Score: _____ / 70 marks

Paper 2

Buck did not read the newspapers, or he would have known that trouble was brewing, not alone for himself, but for every tide-water dog, strong of muscle and with warm, long hair, from Puget Sound to San Diego. Because men, groping in the Arctic darkness, had found a yellow metal, and because steamship and transportation companies were booming the find, thousands of men were rushing into the Northland. These men wanted dogs, and the dogs they wanted were heavy dogs, with strong muscles by which to toil, and furry coats to protect them from the frost.

Buck lived in a big house in the sun-kissed Santa Clara Valley. Judge Miller's place, it was called. It stood back from the road, half hidden among the trees, through which glimpses could be caught of the wide cool veranda that ran around its four sides. The house was approached by gravelled driveways which wound about through wide-spreading lawns and under the interlacing boughs of tall poplars. At the rear things were on even a more spacious scale than at the front. There were great stables, where a dozen grooms and boys held forth, rows of vine-clad servants' cottages, an endless and orderly array of outhouses, long grape arbors, green pastures, orchards, and berry patches. Then there was the pumping plant for the artesian well, and the big cement tank where Judge Miller's boys took their morning plunge and kept cool in the hot afternoon.

And over this great demesne Buck ruled. Here he was born, and here he had lived the four years of his life. It was true, there were other dogs, There could not but be other dogs on so vast a place, but they did not count. They came and went, resided in the populous kennels, or lived obscurely in the recesses of the house after the fashion of Toots, the Japanese pug, or Ysabel, the Mexican hairless,—strange creatures that rarely put nose out of doors or set foot to ground. On the other hand, there were the fox terriers, a score of them at least, who yelped fearful promises at Toots and Ysabel looking out of the windows at them and protected by a legion of housemaids armed with brooms and mops.

But Buck was neither house-dog nor kennel-dog. The whole realm was his. He plunged into the swimming tank or went hunting with the Judge's sons; he escorted Mollie and Alice, the Judge's daughters, on long twilight or early morning rambles; on wintry nights he lay at the Judge's feet before the roaring library fire; he carried the Judge's grandsons on his back, or rolled them in the grass, and guarded their footsteps through wild adventures down to the fountain in the stable yard, and even beyond, where the paddocks were, and the berry patches. Among the terriers he stalked imperiously, and Toots and Ysabel he utterly ignored, for he was king,—king over all creeping, crawling, flying things of Judge Miller's place, humans included.

From *The Call of the Wild* by Jack London

Circle the correct answer.

1. Buck is the name of a:

    a) boy b) man c) dog

    1 mark

2. What breed of dog is Buck?

    _____

    1 mark

3. In your own words, describe how you imagine Buck to look.

    _____
    _____
    _____

    2 marks

4. Which area did Buck live in?

    _____

    1 mark

5. What was the name of the house in which he lived?

    _____

    1 mark

6. Dogs like Buck are needed for a reason. What reason is this? Use evidence from the text to support your answer.

    _____
    _____
    _____
    _____

    4 marks

7. Based on its usage in the passage, what do you think the word **toil** means?

    _____
    _____

    2 marks

8   In your own words describe the house Buck lived in.

    _____

    _____

                                                                    2 marks

9   Based on its usage in the passage, what do you think the word **rear** means?

    _____

                                                                    1 mark

A synonym is a word that means the same as another word. Match the following words with their correct synonym.

10	interlacing	(a)	roomy
11	spacious	(b)	combining
12	rear	(c)	back
13	array	(d)	variety
14	artesian	(e)	craftsman

5 marks

Circle the correct answer.

15 This passage is about:

    a) The importance of dogs in people's lives

    b) Judge Miller's beautiful home

    c) Buck's relationship with Toots and Ysabel

    d) Buck's role within Judge Miller's house

                                                                    1 mark

Complete each word with '**cious**' or '**tious**'.

16 Vi_____

17 Cau_____

18 Mali_____

19 Ficti_____

20 Pre_____

21 Gra_____

22 Spa_____

23 Nutri_____

24 Preten_____

                                                                    9 marks

11

25 In paragraph 3 we are told that the housemaids guard Judge Miller's home. Which quotation from the text tells us this?

_____

_____

_____

2 marks

26 What happens in paragraph 4 of the text? Using your own words write a five sentence summary of this paragraph.

_____

_____

_____

_____

_____

_____

5 marks

27 What do you think happens next? Write a paragraph describing what happens next in the passage. Your paragraph should be written in a similar style to the passage itself.

_____

_____

_____

_____

_____

_____

_____

_____

_____

_____

_____

10 marks

Circle the definition which is nearest in meaning to each of the bolded words below.

28 **toil**
(a) something that can harm other people
(b) something strong that can be used for work
(c) something that can be thrown around

29 **yelped**
(a) to shout at another person
(b) to whisper something to another person
(c) to state something to another person

30 **twilight**
(a) when the sun rises up
(b) when the sun goes down
(c) early in the morning

31 **utterly**
(a) completely
(b) partially
(c) finally

32 **armed**
(a) disarmed
(b) charmed
(c) rendered

33 **glimpses**
(a) stares
(b) glances
(c) gazes

34 **plunge**
(a) dive
(b) race
(c) swoop

7 marks

These words are written in an old-fashioned way. Write them in full.

35 'twas _____

36 o'er _____

37 dimm'd _____

38 'twill _____

39 e'en _____

5 marks

Write a sentence using each of the following words.

40 interlacing _____

41 array _____

42 spacious _____

43 realm _____

44 imperiously _____

45 possibility _____

6 marks

Put the following sentences into plural form, changing any necessary words.

46 I swam in the ocean today.
_____

47 My friend doesn't know how to swim.
_____

48 The cup is too small.
_____

49 I went to school on Saturday.

50 I eat an orange a day.

5 marks

Score: _____ / 70 marks

15

Paper 3

In the times of the Caliph Haroun-al-Raschid there lived in Bagdad a poor porter named Hindbad, who on a very hot day was sent to carry a heavy load from one end of the city to the other. Before he had **accomplished** half the distance he was so tired that, finding himself in a quiet street where the pavement was sprinkled with rose water, and a cool breeze was blowing, he set his burden upon the ground, and sat down to rest in the shade of a grand house. Very soon he decided that he could not have chosen a pleasanter place; a delicious perfume of aloes wood and pastilles came from the open windows and mingled with the scent of the rose water which steamed up from the hot pavement. Within the palace he heard some music, as of many instruments cunningly played, and the melodious warble of nightingales and other birds, and by this, and the appetising smell of many dainty dishes of which he presently became aware, he judged that feasting and merry making were going on. He wondered who lived in this magnificent house which he had never seen before, the street in which it stood being one which he seldom had occasion to pass. To satisfy his curiosity he went up to some splendidly dressed servants who stood at the door, and asked one of them the name of the master of the mansion.

"What," replied he, "do you live in Bagdad, and not know that here lives the noble Sindbad the Sailor, that famous traveller who sailed over every sea upon which the sun shines?"

The porter, who had often heard people speak of the immense wealth of Sindbad, could not help feeling envious of one whose lot seemed to be as happy as his own was miserable. Casting his eyes up to the sky he exclaimed aloud,

"Consider, Mighty Creator of all things, the differences between Sindbad's life and mine. Every day I suffer a thousand hardships and misfortunes, and have hard work to get even enough bad barley bread to keep myself and my family alive, while the lucky Sindbad spends money right and left and lives upon the fat of the land! What has he done that you should give him this pleasant life--what have I done to deserve so hard a fate?"

So saying he stamped upon the ground like one beside himself with misery and despair. Just at this moment a servant came out of the palace, and taking him by the arm said, "Come with me, the noble Sindbad, my master, wishes to speak to you."

Hindbad was not a little surprised at this summons, and feared that his unguarded words might have drawn upon him the displeasure of Sindbad, so he tried to excuse himself upon the pretext that he could not leave the burden which had been entrusted to him in the street. However the lackey promised him that it should be taken care of, and urged him to obey the call so pressingly that at last the porter was obliged to yield.

He followed the servant into a vast room, where a great company was seated round a table covered with all sorts of delicacies. In the place of honour sat a tall, grave man whose long white beard gave him a **venerable** air. Behind his chair stood a crowd of attendants eager to **minister** to his wants. This was the famous Sindbad himself. The porter, more than ever alarmed at the sight of so much magnificence, tremblingly saluted the noble company. Sindbad, making a sign to him to approach, caused him to be seated at his right hand, and himself heaped choice morsels upon his plate, and poured out for him a draught of excellent wine, and presently, when the banquet drew to a close, spoke to him familiarly, asking his name and occupation.

"My lord," replied the porter, "I am called Hindbad."

"I am glad to see you here," continued Sindbad. "And I will answer for the rest of the company that they are equally pleased, but I wish you to tell me what it was that you said just now in the street." For Sindbad, passing by the open window before the feast began, had heard his complaint and therefore had sent for him.

At this question Hindbad was covered with confusion, and hanging down his head, replied, "My lord, I confess that, overcome by weariness and ill-humour, I uttered **indiscreet** words, which I pray you to pardon me."

"Oh!" replied Sindbad, "do not imagine that I am so unjust as to blame you. On the contrary, I understand your situation and can pity you. Only you appear to be mistaken about me, and I wish to set you right. You **doubtless** imagine that I have acquired all the wealth and luxury that you see me enjoy without difficulty or danger, but this is far indeed from being the case. I have only reached this happy state after having for years suffered every possible kind of toil and danger.

"Yes, my noble friends," he continued, addressing the company, "I assure you that my adventures have been strange enough to **deter** even the most **avaricious** men from seeking wealth by **traversing** the seas. Since you have, perhaps, heard but confused accounts of my seven voyages, and the dangers and wonders that I have met with by sea and land, I will now give you a full and true account of them, which I think you will be well pleased to hear."

As Sindbad was relating his adventures chiefly on account of the porter, he ordered, before beginning his tale, that the burden which had been left in the street should be carried by some of his own servants to the place for which Hindbad had set out at first, while he remained to listen to the story.

From *The Seven Voyages of Sindbad The Sailor* by Andrew Lang

1. Based on the information given in the passage, what does a porter do?

_____
_____

1 mark

2. Why did Hindbad have to stop for a rest before he finished his task?

_____
_____
_____

2 marks

'Very soon he (Hindbad) decided that he could not have chosen a pleasanter place (to take a rest)…' The word 'pleasanter' is a comparative adjective. Comparative adjectives are used when we compare two things. Fill in the blanks with comparative adjectives.

3. tall - _____
4. slim - _____
5. good - _____
6. bad - _____
7. tidy - _____

5 marks

8. What made Hindbad conclude that there was feasting and merry-making in the house?

_____
_____
_____

2 marks

9. Why was it that Hindbad had never seen the house before?

_____
_____
_____

2 marks

10. Circle the correct answer.

According to the servant of the house, Sindbad the Sailor was a famous traveller who 'sailed over every sea upon which the sun shines'. This means that Sindbad the Sailor…

(a) only sailed in the day when the sun was up.
(b) travelled widely.
(c) only travelled when the weather was fair.

1 mark

11   Sindbad the Sailor was known to possess 'immense wealth.' Find another word in the passage that has the same meaning as the word 'immense'.

   _____

   1 mark

A **hyperbole** is a form of exaggeration that is meant to emphasise a point. For example, Hindbad lamented that everyday he suffered 'a thousand hardships and misfortunes'. Complete the following hyperboles with the words and phrases provided.

| tonne | cats and dogs | mile | fortune | horse |

12   It was raining _____ when Sally was finally able to leave for the day.
13   Eric could smell the apple pie baking from a _____ away.
14   This house must have cost the Smiths a _____.
15   Henry was so hungry he was sure he could eat a _____.
16   The bag was so heavy that Carrie thought it must have weighed a _____.

5 marks

Hindbad lamented that lucky Sindbad 'spent money right and left' and 'lived upon the fat of the land'. In you own words, explain what these phrases mean.

17   Spent money left and right:

   _____

18   Lived upon the fat of the land:

   _____

4 marks

19   When Sindbad summoned Hindbad, Hindbad tried to excuse himself. Why did Hindbad try to excuse himself? Support your answer with evidence from the story.

   _____
   _____
   _____
   _____
   _____

4 marks

20   How did Sindbad treat Hindbad during the banquet? Support your answer with two pieces of evidence from the passage.

   _____
   _____
   _____
   _____
   _____

4 marks

21 Was Sindbad a young or old man when Hindbad met him? Support your answer with evidence from the passage.

_____
_____
_____
_____

3 marks

22 Do you think Sindbad was angry with Hindbad for making the assumption that Sindbad had acquired his wealth and luxury without difficulty or danger? Support your answer with two pieces of evidence from the passage.

_____
_____
_____
_____
_____

4 marks

23 How do you think Hindbad reacted after hearing Sindbad's story? Support your answer with evidence from the story.

_____
_____
_____
_____
_____

4 marks

24 How would you describe Hindbad? Use an adjective to describe Hindbad's character and support your answer with evidence from the extract.

_____
_____
_____
_____

3 marks

Adverbs are used to modify verbs. They tell us when, where, how, in what manner, or to what extent an action is performed. Complete the sentences with the adverbs provided.

| cunningly | splendidly | pressingly | tremblingly | familiarly | chiefly |

25 Although the two friends had not seen each other for years, they spoke to each other _____ and it was as if they had never lost touch with each other.

26 One of the young ladies at the debutant ball was more _____ attired than the rest, and wore a bejewelled tiara in her hair.

27 The most pressing agenda of the conference was to draft an agreement that will limit global warming, _____ by reducing greenhouse gas emissions.

28 The sly fox _____ lured the rabbit into his lair.
29 Three months into his gap year, Terry discovered that his funds were running dangerously low and wrote _____ to his parents, hoping that they would be able to send him some money.
30 The servant _____ swept up the shards of broken glass and shot out of the study before his master could lose his temper and throw another glass in his direction.

6 marks

A collective noun is a word for a group of specific items, animals or people. For example, during the banquet, there was <u>a crowd of</u> attendants standing behind Sindbad's chair, eager to minister to his wants. Fill in the blanks with the words given to complete the collective nouns.

| network | line | crash | murder | host |

31 A _____ of rhinoceroses
32 A _____ of computers
33 A _____ of crows
34 A _____ of angels
35 A _____ of kings

5 marks

Circle the definition which is nearest in meaning to the bolded word as it is used in the passage.

36 **accomplished**
(a) highly skilled
(b) achieved
(c) completed

37 **venerable**
(a) someone who is revered
(b) someone who is religious
(c) someone who is extremely wealthy

38 **minister**
(a) to act as a political representative
(b) to act as a representative of a religion
(c) to attend to the needs of someone

39 **indiscreet**
(a) lacking empathy
(b) lacking good judgement

(c) lacking content

40 doubtless
(a) recklessly
(b) naively
(c) unquestionably

41 deter
(a) discourage
(b) encourage
(c) enable

42 avaricious
(a) adventurous
(b) courageous
(c) materialistic

43 traversing
(a) lying across
(b) travelling across
(c) looking over

8 marks

A **prefix** is placed at the beginning of a word to modify or change its meaning. Fill in the blanks with the prefixes provided.

ab -	ad -	ante -	be -	com -	counter -	de -

44 _____act
45 _____duct
46 _____stract
47 _____cedent
48 _____witch
49 _____bat
50 _____brief

7 marks

Score: _____ / 70 marks

Paper 4

I have a little shadow that goes in and out with me,

And what can be the use of him is more than I can see.

He is very, very like me from the heels up to the head;

And I see him jump before me, when I jump into my bed.

The funniest thing about him is the way he likes to grow—

Not at all like proper children, which is always very slow;

For he sometimes shoots up taller like an india-rubber ball,

And he sometimes gets so little that there's none of him at all.

He hasn't got a notion of how children ought to play,

And can only make a fool of me in every sort of way.

He stays so close beside me, he's a coward you can see;

I'd think shame to stick to nursie as that shadow sticks to me!

One morning, very early, before the sun was up,

I rose and found the shining dew on every buttercup;

But my lazy little shadow, like an arrant sleepy-head,

Had stayed at home behind me and was fast asleep in bed.

My Shadow by Robert Louis Stevenson

From Stanza 1

1. Do you think the poet is a boy or a girl? Support your answer with evidence from the poem.

   _____

   _____

   _____

   _____

   3 marks

2. How is it possible that the poet saw the shadow jump into bed before he/she jumps into bed? Explain your answer.

   _____

   _____

   _____

   _____

   4 marks

An **antonym** is a word which is **opposite** in meaning to another.

Example: 'I have a little shadow that goes **in** and **out** with me…'

Fill in the blanks with the correct antonyms for the following words.

3. absent: _____

4. backwards: _____

5. clean: _____

6. dangerous: _____

7. empty: _____

5 marks

Prepositions are words that tell us about the position, direction or place of an object or person.

Example: 'And I see him jump **before** me, when I jump **into** my bed...'

Circle the most appropriate preposition in each sentence.

8   Terry was surprised to see what was (at, inside, on) the box when he opened it.

9   The performer balanced himself (with, above, on) the tight-rope.

10 The painter reminded us not to lean (on, beside, against) the wall which has just been painted.

11 The bullet-train shot (through, over, in) the tunnel at lightning speed.

12 The police announced that one of the criminals had escaped (in, from, to) prison the night before.

5 marks

From Stanza 2

Circle the correct answer.

13 According to the poet, the shadow grows very:

(a) slowly

(b) quickly

1 mark

14 At what part of the day (dawn, morning, afternoon, evening, night, etc) does the shadow "shoot[s] up taller like an india-rubber ball"?

_____

1 mark

26

15 At what part of the day (dawn, morning, afternoon, evening, night, etc) does the shadow "get[s] so little that there's none of him at all"?

_____

1 mark

Superlatives are used to express the highest degree when three or more things or persons are compared.

Example: 'The **funniest** thing about him is the way he likes to grow…'

Fill in the blanks with the correct superlatives.

16 able, abler, _____

17 bright, brighter, _____

18 cruel, crueller, _____

19 dim, dimmer, _____

20 eerie, eerier, _____

5 marks

An **indefinite pronoun** does not refer to any specific person, thing or amount. It is vague and "not definite". Some indefinite pronouns include: some, any, none.

Example: 'And he sometimes gets so little that there's **none** of him at all…'

Complete the sentences with the following pronouns: **some, any, none**.

21 Where are the potatoes? There should be _____ in the pantry.

22 Fred came home empty-handed. He had _____ of the items his wife had instructed him to pick up from the supermarket.

23 Those are _____ of the photographs the proud father had taken of his newborn-daughter recently.

24 Please remember to bring back the change if there is _____.

25 The couple looked at many honeymoon packages. However, _____ of

27

them took their fancy.

5 marks

From Stanza 3 and 4

26 How would you describe the poet's impression of his/her shadow? Support your answer with evidence from the poem.

_____

_____

_____

_____

4 marks

27 In your opinion, why do you think the poet's shadow was still "fast asleep" in bed when the poet was already awake?

_____

_____

_____

_____

4 marks

28 What do you think was the poet's response when he found the shadow still fast asleep in bed when he was already up? Explain your answer.

_____

_____

_____

_____

3 marks

A **contraction** is a word that has been shortened. It is usually made by joining two words and leaving out one or more letters. An apostrophe (') replaces the letter or letters that are left out.

Example: 'He **hasn't** got a notion of how children ought to play.'

Rewrite the following sentences using contractions instead of the underlined words.

29 Linda does not like children.

30 My mother cannot cook well.

31 They would come if they could.

32 Benjamin could not complete the questions.

33 They had better ask for permission before they leave for the day.

5 marks

Modal verbs are used to show whether something is certain, probable or possible. We also use modals to do things like talking about ability, asking permission, making requests and offers, etc.

Example: 'He doesn't have a notion of how children **ought to** play…'

Other examples of modal verbs include: can, could, may, might, shall, should, will, would, must.

Fill in the blanks with the modal verbs provided in the box.

should	must	ought to

34 You _____ eat more fruits and vegetables because it can make you healthier.

35 Drivers _____ stop for pedestrians at marked crossings. It's against the law for drivers not to do so.

36 In order to vote in the elections, you _____ go in person to the polling station.

37 I think you _____ go home since you are sick.

29

38 You _____ admit that you made a mistake. You know it's the right thing to do.

5 marks

39 From its usage in the passage, what do you think the word **arrant** means?

_____

1 mark

From all stanzas

A **rhyme** is a repetition of similar sounds (or the same sound) in two or more words.

Example: 'But my lazy little shadow, like an arrant sleepy-**head**, / Had stayed at home behind me and was fast asleep in **bed**…'

Find a word from the poem that rhymes with the following word:

40 dead: _____

41 sway: _____

42 fall: _____

3 marks

43 What do you think happens next? Write a four-line stanza describing what happens between the poet and his/her shadow. Your paragraph should be written in a similar style to the earlier stanzas and should also include rhyming patterns similar to those in earlier stanzas.

_____

_____

_____

_____

_____

8 marks

Rewrite and punctuate each of the following sentences carefully.

44 make sure you dont drive over the speed limit mr jones cautioned his son henry

45 goodness how could such a tragedy have happened asked Karen when she heard about the plane crash

46 andrew please come over here and take a seat said the headmaster there is something I would like to speak to you about

47 i wouldnt have lost my job if id taken your advice lamented ian to graham

48 don't touch that kettle its hot shouted mrs rogers to her son

49 only Pamela and i went to the party mary did not go said janet

50 as their shoes were very muddy they were not allowed to come into the room explained the teacher

7 marks

Score: _____ / 70 marks

Paper 5

It was the Feast of the New Year, the oldest and most splendid of all the feasts in the Kingdom of Persia, and the day had been spent by the king in the city of Schiraz, taking part in the magnificent spectacles prepared by his subjects to do honour to the festival. The sun was setting, and the monarch was about to give his court the signal to retire, when suddenly a strange man appeared before his throne, leading a horse richly harnessed, and looking in every respect exactly like a real one.

"Sire," said he, prostrating himself as he spoke, "although I make my appearance so late before your Highness, I can confidently assure you that none of the wonders you have seen during the day can be compared to this horse, if you will deign to cast your eyes upon him."

"I see nothing in it," replied the king, "except a clever imitation of a real one; and any skilled workman might do as much."

"Sire," he stated, "it is not of his outward form that I would speak, but of the use that I can make of him. I have only to mount him, and to wish myself in some special place, and no matter how distant it may be, in a very few moments I shall find myself there. It is this, Sire, that makes the horse so marvellous, and if your Highness will allow me, you can prove it for yourself."

The King of Persia had never before come across a horse with such qualities, asked the stranger to mount the animal and show what he could do. In an instant the man had vaulted on his back, and inquired where the monarch wished to send him.

"Do you see that mountain?" asked the king, pointing to a huge mass that towered into the sky about three leagues from Schiraz; "go and bring me the leaf of a palm that grows at the foot."

The words were hardly out of the king's mouth when the man turned a screw placed in the horse's neck, close to the saddle, and the animal bounded like lightning up into the air, and was soon beyond the sight even of the sharpest eyes. In a quarter of an hour the strange man was seen returning, bearing in his hand the palm, and, guiding his horse to the foot of the throne, he dismounted, and laid the leaf before the king.

Now the monarch had no sooner proved the astonishing speed of which the horse was capable than he longed to possess it himself, and indeed, so sure was he that the man would be quite ready to sell it, that he looked upon it as his own already.

"I never guessed from his mere outside how valuable an animal he was," he remarked to the man, "and I am grateful to you for having shown me my error," said he. "If you will sell it, name your own price."

"Sire," replied the man, "I never doubted that a sovereign so wise and accomplished as your Highness would do justice to my horse, when he once knew its power; and I even went so far as to think it probable that you might wish to possess it. Greatly as I prize it, I will yield.

From *The Enchanted Horse* by Andrew Lang

1. Why do you think the King of Persia had to spend the day taking part in the festivities instead of spending it in his palace?

_____

_____

_____

_____

3 marks

Capital letters are used in the first letters of proper nouns.

Example: 'It was the **Feast** of the **New Year**, the oldest and most splendid of all the feasts in the **Kingdom of Persia**, and the day had been spent by the king in the city of **Schiraz**...'

Rewrite the following sentence, taking care to use capital letters for proper nouns.

2. rachael will be spending christmas in spain this year.

3. i have a dental appointment with dr jones on thursday.

4. mrs. harper told us during class today that the tiniest country in the world is the vatican city.

5. george likes to use google when he surfs the internet, but his brother gary prefers yahoo.

6. the atlantic ocean isn't as big as the pacific ocean, but both oceans are bigger than the Indian ocean.

5 marks

7. At which part of the day (dawn, afternoon, dusk, night) did the man appear before the king? Support your answer with evidence from the passage.

_____

_____

_____

2 marks

8. From its usage in the passage, what do you think the word '**prostrate**' means?

_____

1 mark

9 Why do you think the stranger prostrated himself as he addressed the king? Explain your answer.

_____
_____
_____

2 marks

10 Was the horse that the stranger presented a real horse? Support your answer with evidence from the passage.

_____
_____
_____

2 marks

11 In your own words, describe two aspects you notice about the stranger's attitude when he spoke to the king about his horse. Support your answer with evidence from the passage.

_____
_____
_____
_____
_____

5 marks

12 Did the horse move very quickly or very slowly? Support your answer with evidence from the passage.

_____
_____
_____

3 marks

Circle the correct answer.

13 After seeing what the horse could do, the king was (keen, not keen) to purchase the horse for himself.

1 mark

14 After reading the passage, do you think the stranger will sell the horse to the king? Explain your answer with evidence from the passage.

_____

_____

_____

_____

3 marks

15 Put the following sentences in the correct order by writing the number that corresponds to the correct order in the following blanks.

(a) The strange man beseeched the king to allow him to demonstrate the horse's capabilities. _____

(b) He laid the leaf before the king. _____

(c) The man turned a screw placed in the horse's neck and set off. _____

(d) He explained to the king that this was an enchanted horse and it could travel to any place its rider desired in a very short time. _____

(e) The king requested that the man bring him the leaf of a palm that grows at the foot of a mountain three leagues from the city of Schiraz. _____

(f) A strange man appeared before the King of Persia on the day of the Feast of the New Year with a horse. _____

(g) In a quarter of an hour, he was back with the leaf the king requested. _____

7 marks

Complete each of the following words with letters 'el' or 'le'.

16 tow_ _

17 scramb_ _

18 wrink_ _ d

19 squirr_ _

20 tab_ _

35

21   cam_ _

22   trav_ _

23   cand_ _

7 marks

24   After reading the passage, what do you think was the stranger's motive for presenting the horse to the King of Persia? Explain your answer using evidence from the passage if necessary.

_____

_____

_____

_____

3 marks

Fiction refers to literature that is a work of the imagination and not necessarily based on fact. However, non-fiction refers to literature that presents real-life events, established facts, and true information.

25   After reading the passage, would you classify the story as fiction or non-fiction? Explain your answer drawing evidence from the passage if necessary.

_____

_____

_____

_____

4 marks

Circle the definition which is nearest in meaning to the bolded word as it is used in the passage.

26   **magnificent**

(a)   significant

(b)   unimportant

(c)   splendid

27   **spectacles**

(a)   eyeglasses

(b)   displays

(c) illustrations

28 **retire**
(a) to abandon
(b) to go to bed
(c) to withdraw

29 **harnessed**
(a) saddled
(b) decorated
(c) strapped

30 **deign**
(a) to oppose
(b) to consent
(c) to commit

31 **mount**
(a) to increase in intensity
(b) to drop down to
(c) to get up on

32 **bade**
(a) commanded
(b) urged
(c) offered

33 **distant**
(a) close to
(b) removed from
(c) far off

8 marks

Write a sentence using each of the following words:

34 mass

_____

35 astonishing

_____

36 possess

_____

37 error

_____

38 yield

_____

5 marks

Relative pronouns are used to join two sentences, or to give more information about something. Examples of relative pronouns include who, which, that, whom, whose.

Fill in the blanks with the relative pronouns provided.

| who | whose | whom | which | that |

39 The singer _____ was injured in an accident, will not be performing in the concert next month.

40 The books _____ have red covers are new.

41 The man _____ car has broken down, is now trying to flag down a taxi.

42 Is this the bakery _____ sells pastries at half price after 9 p.m.?

43 Leap years, _____ have 366 days, contain an extra day in February.

44 The lady _____ purse was snatched, is a friend of mine.

45 Please return the book to _____ it belongs instead of simply leaving it on the table.

7 marks

Fill in each blank with the plural form of the word in brackets.

46 Those _____ (apple) were sweet and juicy.

47 About a hundred _____ (sheep) were grazing on the hillside.

48 The _____ (child) were warned not to play near the construction site.

49 The _____ (thief) were caught and handed over to the police.

50 The _____ (princess) were waited upon by their servants.

_____
5 marks

Score: _____ / 70 marks

Answer Guide

Paper 1

1 (c)

1 mark

2 (b)

1 mark

3 The shoe could not be found on the stairs, hall, garden, henhouse, kennel or meadow.

5 marks

4 The two adjectives are "glimmering" and "dark."

1 mark

5 The adjectives are effective because they give more information about the nouns used in the poem. The adjectives also help readers to form a better visual image by enabling them to picture what happens. For instance, the adjective "glimmering" gives a luminous quality to the moon and the adjective "dark" gives a sinister and dangerous quality to the description of the sea.

1 mark

6 I would describe Lucy as being very unlucky because she can't find her shoe anywhere.

2 marks

7 patter

1 mark

8 The moon is shiny and luminous.

9 The ships moved across dangerous seas.

10 Showed no signs of.

11 In a building that houses pigeons and doves.

2 marks

40

12   The alliterative expression is "did dance."

1 mark

13   e (compliment)

14   e (shingle)

15   s (mischance)

16   s (lost)

17   s (desire)

18   s (astray)

19   e (forgotten)

20   ss (missing)

8 marks

21   This poem is about a girl called Lucy who lost her shoe. She looked for her shoe in the house but could not find it. She extended the search to the compound outside the house but could not find it either. Despite looking beyond the house and its surroundings, she still couldn't find her shoe.

4 marks

(a) This idiom is used to extract information from someone who is being very quiet.

(b) It is your turn to act or respond to the situation.

(c) To enjoy the benefits of two different things at the same time.

(d) To take on more responsibilities than you can handle.

(e) This refers to something that is very expensive.

(f) To pointlessly lament about a misfortune that cannot be undone.

(g) This idiom encourages people to not put all their energy into one opportunity and to be open to accepting several opportunities at the same time.

(h) To hear something informally through gossip or rumour.

(i) To leave out non-essential parts of a story so that it is shorter and to the point.

(j) Not to take something literally.

10 marks

22 The idioms that the student has written down should be real idioms and not made-up ones.

Examples might include any of the following:

By hook or by crook, to bury the hatchet, to call a spade a spade, to spin a yarn, to have a bone to pick.

5 marks

23 He sat <u>silently</u> during dinner.

24 She played <u>roughly</u> during playtime.

25 Joe and I go to football practice <u>daily</u>.

3 marks

26 (d)   7 marks

27 (c)

28 (b)

29 (e)

30 (a)

5 marks

31 h (thief)

32 h (lightning)

33 p (publication)

34 pp (approval)

35 p (hamper)

36 p (centipede)

42

37 h (shakily)

38 h (handler)

39 p (proportion)

40 h (hospital)

10 marks

41 ugly

42 after

43 reject

44 forward

45 agitated

46 lend

47 appear

48 broad

49 incorrect

50 bold

10 marks

Paper 2

1 (c)

1 mark

2 Buck is a tide-water dog.

1 mark

3 I think Buck is quite a large dog with a sturdy build. He also has long fur.

2 marks

4 Buck lived in Santa Clara Valley.

1 mark

5 The house he lived in was known as Judge Miller's place.

1 mark

6 According to the information in the passage, men who were mining yellow metal (gold) were rushing into the Northland and they needed strong dogs like Buck to work hard alongside them. This therefore suggests that such dogs were needed to help pull sleighs that carry equipment because they were strong and could withstand the cold. They might even be used as rescue dogs for men lost in the snow and ice.

4 marks

7 The word "toil" means to work hard.

2 marks

8 Buck lived in a grand house that had a broad terrace around its sides. At the front of the house there were wide lawns and tall trees. There were stables for horses, housing for staff, green pastures, orchards and berry patches, and a big cement tank that served as a small pool.

2 marks

9 The word "rear" means the back of the house Buck lived in.

1 marks

10 (b)

11 (a)

12 (c)

13 (d)

14 (e)

5 marks

15 (d)

1 mark

16 cious

17 tious

18 cious

19 tious

20 cious

21 cious

22 cious

23 tious

24 tious

9 marks

25 The phrase 'protected by a legion of housemaids armed with brooms and mops' tells us that the housemaids guard Judge Miller's home.

2 marks

26 Buck was part of the family at Judge Miller's place. He accompanied the judge's sons when they swam and hunted, escorted the judge's daughters, and kept the judge company in the library. He even played with the judge's grandsons and looked out for them as they played in the vast compound of the house. Although there were other dogs at Judge Miller's place, Buck ignored them all and behaved as if he was king.

5 marks

27 *Students' answers may vary.*

10 marks

28 (b)

29 (a)

30 (b)

31 (a)

32 (c)

33 (b)

34 (a)

7 marks

35 it was

36 over

37 dimmed

38 it will

39 even

5 marks

40 From the hill, he had a clear view of the countryside and could see many little streams overlapping and <u>interlacing</u> one with another to form an intricate pattern.

41 The excited bride-to-be was overwhelmed by the dazzling <u>array</u> of choices for a wedding at the bridal tradeshow.

42 The sitting room of the grand house was a <u>spacious</u> dwelling that contained a huge fireplace, a grand piano and clusters of comfortable couches and armchairs arranged in intimate circles.

43 The kind-hearted king offered shelter and assistance in his <u>realm</u> for those who were driven out of their homeland in the neighbouring countries due to war and natural disasters.

44 The haughty prefect looked <u>imperiously</u> at the latecomer and reached for his little notebook to book him.

46

45 Andy was disappointed that he had missed the application date by a month and there was no possibility of taking the entrance examinations until the next academic year.

6 marks

46 We swam in the ocean today.

47 Our friends don't know how to swim.

48 The cups are too small.

49 We went to school on Saturday.

50 We eat an orange a day. / We eat oranges on a daily basis.

5 marks

Paper 3

1 Based the information in the passage, a porter's job is to carry heavy things from one place to another.

1 mark

2 Hindbad had to stop for a rest before he finished his task because it was a very hot day and he had to carry an extremely heavy load.

2 marks

3 taller

4 slimmer

5 better

6 worse

7 tidier

5 marks

8 Hindbad concluded that there was feasting and merry-making in the house because he heard music and smelled the aroma of delicious food from within the palace.

2 marks

9 Hindbad had never seen the house before because the house was located in a street that he had never had to opportunity to visit.

2 marks

10 (b)

1 mark

11 The word in the passage that has the same meaning as 'immense' is 'vast.'

1 mark

12 cats and dogs

13 mile

14 fortune

48

15 horse

16 tonne

5 marks

17 It means when someone spends money at every opportunity

18 It refers to when someone has enough money to lead a comfortable life without having to work.

4 marks

19 Hindbad tried to excuse himself from having to meet Sindbad because prior to being summoned by Sindbad, he had been lamenting on how lucky Sindbad was to be able to enjoy all the wealth without having to work hard for it. Hindbad was worried that Sindbad had heard his remarks, was angry with him and had hence summoned Hindbad to reprimand him. Hindbad therefore wanted to excuse himself so that he would not offend Sindbad further.

Evidence from the source can come from either direct quotations or by reference to the text.

4 marks

20 Sindbad treated Hindbad politely and respectfully. He invited Hindbad to sit on his right at the dining table, personally picked out the best parts of the delicacies and put them on Sindbad's plate. Sindbad also poured wine for Hindbad and as the banquet drew to a close, spoke to Hindbad in a friendly manner and asked him his name and occupation.

The two pieces of evidence from the source can come from either direct quotations or by reference to the text.

4 marks

21 Sindbad was an old man when Hindbad met him. When Hindbad set eyes on Sindbad, he saw that Sindbad had a long white beard. His servant had also mentioned to Hindbad that Sindbad had travelled very widely and Sindbad himself revealed that he had only come to accumulate his wealth after many years of suffering. Hence, this this tells readers that Sindbad was an old man when Hindbad met him.

Evidence from the source can come from either direct quotations or by reference to the text.

3 marks

22 Sindbad was not angry with Hindbad for making the assumption that he had acquired his wealth and luxury without difficulty or danger. When Hindbad confessed that he had been indiscreet with his words, instead of using strong words, Sindbad assured Hindbad that he did not blame him for making such remarks. He explained to Hindbad that he understood why Sindbad had made the assumption and even offered to share the story of how he became wealthy.

Evidence from the source can come from either direct quotations or by reference to the text.

4 marks

23 I think after hearing Sindbad's story, Hindbad might feel ashamed about having assumed that Sindbad had come into his wealth without having to work hard for it and might apologise for the insensitive and indiscreet remarks he had made earlier. Before sharing his story to Hindbad, Sindbad mentioned that he had only reached this happy state after having suffered every possible kind of toil and danger. He also mentioned that his adventures were strange enough to discourage even the most adventurous men from seeking wealth.

Evidence from the source can come from either direct quotations or by reference to the text.

4 marks

24 I think Hindbad is a cowardly man. When he was summoned by Sindbad, he was afraid that his remarks might have angered Sindbad and he therefore tried to avoid confrontation with him by saying that he had to see the load that had been entrusted to him. I therefore think that Hindbad was a gutless and spineless man who was afraid of offending someone rich and powerful.

Evidence from the source can come from either direct quotations or by reference to the text.

3 marks

25 familiarly

26 splendidly

27 chiefly

28 cunningly

29 pressingly

30 tremblingly

                                                                        5 marks

31 crash

32 network

33 murder

34 host

35 line

                                                                         5 marks

36 (b)

37 (a)

38 (c)

39 (b)

40 (c)

41 (a)

42 (c)

43 (b)

                                                                         8 marks

44 <u>counter</u>act

45 <u>de</u>duct

46 <u>ab</u>stract

47 <u>ante</u>cedent

48 <u>be</u>witch

49 <u>com</u>bat

50 <u>de</u>brief

51

                                                                    7 marks

Paper 4

1   I think that the poet is a boy. This is because the poet used words such as 'he' and 'him' when referring to the shadow. He also says, "he is very, very like me" which suggests that the poet is the same gender as the shadow and is therefore male.

                                                                    3 marks

2   This is possible if the poet's bed is facing a window. When the poet stands between his bed and the window and when the sun is at the right position, the poet's shadow would fall on the bed. Hence it would seem as if the poet's shadow jumped before him when he jumped into bed.

                                                                    4 marks

3   present

4   forwards

5   dirty

6   safe

7   full

                                                                    5 marks

8   inside

9   on

10 against

11 through

12 from

                                                                    5 marks

13 (b)

                                                                    1 mark

52

14 The shadow shoots up taller like an Indian-rubber ball in the morning.

   at dawn and in the evening are also acceptable answers.

   1 mark

15 The shadow gets so little that there is none of him at all in the afternoon.

   1 mark

16 ablest

17 brightest

18 cruellest

19 dimmest

20 eeriest

   5 marks

21 some

22 none

23 some

24 any

25 none

   5 marks

26 The poet did not seem to like his shadow very much and seemed to talk about his shadow in a condescending manner. For instance, the poet talked negatively about his shadow and said that his shadow made a fool out of him in every sort of way. The poet also called his shadow a "coward" for sticking close to him.

   4 marks

27 I think there was a window in front of the port's bed in his bedroom. When the poet woke up at in the morning and stood before the window, the shadow cast by the morning sun fell onto the bed. Hence it appeared as if the poet's shadow was still in bed and "asleep" although the poet was already up.

   4 marks

28 I think the poet would not be very happy and might talk negatively about his shadow or might even reprimand his shadow for being in bed when the poet was already up. From the earlier parts of the poem, it is clear that poet did not seem to talk positively about the shadow. The poet referred to his shadow as a coward, claimed that his shadow made a fool of him in every way and also called his shadow an "arrant sleepy-head."

3 marks

29 doesn't

30 can't

31 They'd

32 couldn't

33 They'd

5 marks

34 ought to

35 must

36 must

37 should

38 ought to

5 marks

39 From its usage in the poem, the word 'arrant' means total / complete/outright.

1 mark

40 head

41 play or way

42 All or ball

3 marks

43 *Answers vary from student to student*

8 marks

54

44 "Make sure you don't drive over the speed limit," Mr. Jones cautioned his son, Henry.

45 "Goodness! How could such a tragedy have happened?" asked Karen when she heard about the plane crash.

46 "Andrew, please come over here and take a seat," said the headmaster. "There's something I would like to speak to you about."

47 "I wouldn't have lost my job if I'd taken your advice," lamented Ian to Graham.

48 "Don't touch that kettle! It's hot!" shouted Mrs. Rogers to her son.

49 "Only Pamela and I went to the party. Mary did not go," said Janet.

50 "As their shoes were very muddy, they were not allowed to come into the room," explained the teacher.

7 marks

Paper 5

1. The king had to spend the day taking part in the festivities instead of spending it in his palace because it was the Feast of the New Year, the most splendid of all the festivals in the kingdom and the king's subjects had prepared spectacular displays to honour the festival. The king therefore had to take part in the festivities and celebrate the day with the people.

3 marks

2. Rachel will be spending Christmas in Spain this year.

3. I have a dental appointment with Dr. Jones on Thursday.

4. Mrs. Harper told us during class today that the tiniest country in the world is the Vatican City.

5. George likes to use Google when he surfs the Internet, but his brother Gary prefers Yahoo.

6. The Atlantic Ocean isn't as big as the Pacific Ocean, but both oceans are bigger than the Indian Ocean.

5 marks

7. The man appeared before the king at dusk. According to the information in the passage, the sun was setting, and the king was about to give his court the signal to withdraw, when suddenly the man appeared before the king.

2 marks

8. Based on its usage in the passage, to 'prostrate' means to kneel down on the ground, with the face down.

1 mark

9. I think the stranger prostrated himself as he addressed the king as a sign of respect and humility.

2 marks

10. According to the information in the passage, the stranger presented a horse that was richly harnessed, and it looked very much like a real horse. This therefore tells us that the horse that the stranger presented to the king was not real.

2 marks

11   The stranger was very respectful and humble as he spoke to the king about his horse. The stranger prostrated himself and he respectfully addressed the king as "sire." He also appeared to be very confident about the horse's capabilities. For instance, the stranger assured the king that none of the wonders he had seen during the festivities of the day could be compared to the horse. Furthermore, he spoke to the king in a flattering manner. For example, he praised the king's wisdom in recognising the horse's abilities and said that he never doubted that a sovereign as wise and accomplished as the king would do justice to the horse.

5 marks

12   The horse moved very quickly. According to the information from the passage, when the king requested that the stranger and the horse travelled to the mountain and bring back a palm leaf, the horse bounded like lightning up into the air, and was soon beyond sight. In a quarter of an hour the strange man and the horse returned, with the palm leaf.

3 marks

13   keen

1 mark

14   I think the stranger will sell the horse to the king, or perhaps ask for something from the king in exchange for the horse. According to the information from the passage, the stranger was very eager to show the king what the horse could do. It was possible that the stranger was eager to prove the capabilities of the horse so that the king would be tempted to buy it. The stranger said that he thought it was possible that the king might want to possess it, and he also said that he would yield to the king's request.

3 marks

15

(a)   3

(b)   7

(c)   5

(d)   2

(e) 4

(f) 1

(g) 6

7 marks

16 tow<u>el</u>

17 scramb<u>le</u>

18 wrink<u>led</u>

19 squirr<u>el</u>

20 tab<u>le</u>

21 cam<u>el</u>

22 trav<u>el</u>

23 cand<u>le</u>

7 marks

24 I think the stranger's motive for presenting the horse to the King of Persia was to get the king to buy the horse from him, or to get the king to offer him something he wanted in exchange for the horse. He was also quick to prove the capabilities of the horse to the king. In addition, the stranger praised the king's wisdom and said that he would yield if the king wanted the horse. This indicates that the stranger was keen to leave a good impression on the king.

3 marks

25 I would classify the story as fiction because the story features magical and mysterious elements that are not based on facts. For instance, the stranger suddenly appeared before the king's throne; or a horse that looked real and could fly at an astonishing speed. This suggests that the story is based on the author's imagination which makes it a fictional story.

4 marks

26 (c)

27 (b)

28 (c)

58

29 (a)

30 (b)

31 (c)

32 (a)

33 (c)

    8 marks

34 Even from a distance, the driver could see a black <u>mass</u> in the road.

35 She watched in amazement as the usually languid man rushed at his opponent with <u>astonishing</u> speed.

36 The recipes <u>posses</u> an innovative approach to preparing vegetarian food.

37 He was unfortunately far too arrogant to learn the <u>error</u> of his ways and continued to ignore the advice of those who wished he would turn over a new leaf.

38 Fearing for the safety of his daughter, the wealthy man <u>yielded</u> to the demands of the kidnappers and paid the ransom without informing the police.

    5 marks

39 who

40 that

41 whose

42 that

43 which

44 whose

45 whom

    7 marks

46 apples

47 sheep

48 children

59

49 thieves

50 princesses

5 marks

DOWNLOAD FREE WORKSHEETS

&

EDUCATIONAL RESOURCES

Sign up for free educational resources at
http://www.thetutoress.com/resources

Copyright © 2015 Miss Olubi & TheTutoress.com

All rights reserved. This book or any portion thereof may not be reproduced or used in any matter whatsoever without the express written permission of the publisher.

Printed in Great Britain
by Amazon